What if one small choice had the power to
CHANGE THE WORLD?

For Evan. You make the world better. —E.B.

For all those who with a simple act
take care of planet Earth. —M.Á.M.

Text copyright © 2022 by Elisa Boxer
Jacket art and interior illustrations copyright © 2022 by Marta Álvarez Miguéns

All rights reserved. Published in the United States by Crown Books for Young Readers,
an imprint of Random House Children's Books, a division of Penguin Random House LLC, New York.

Crown and the colophon are registered trademarks of Penguin Random House LLC.

Visit us on the Web! rhcbooks.com

Educators and librarians, for a variety of teaching tools, visit us at
RHTeachersLibrarians.com

Library of Congress Cataloging-in-Publication Data
Names: Boxer, Elisa, author. | Álvarez Miguéns, Marta, illustrator.
Title: One turtle's last straw : the real-life rescue that sparked a sea change / written by Elisa Boxer ; illustrated by Marta Álvarez Miguéns.
Description: First edition. | New York : Crown Books for Young Readers, [2022] | Includes bibliographical references. |
Audience: Ages 4–8 | Audience: Grades K–1 |
Summary: "Based on the viral video that set a movement in motion, this heart-wrenching story of one turtle's rescue
reminds us that even the smallest straw can hurt our ocean life—and that the smallest demand for change
can grow into something big!" –Provided by publisher.
Identifiers: LCCN 2021043162 (print) | LCCN 2021043163 (ebook) |
ISBN 978-0-593-37246-3 (hardcover) | ISBN 978-0-593-37247-0 (library binding) |
ISBN 978-0-593-37248-7 (ebook)
Subjects: LCSH: Turtles—Anecdotes—Juvenile literature. |
Marine biodiversity conservation—Juvenile literature. | Plastic marine debris—Environmental aspects—Juvenile literature. |
Drinking straws—Environmental aspects—Juvenile literature.
Classification: LCC QL795.T8 B69 2022 (print) | LCC QL795.T8 (ebook) |
DDC 597.92—dc23

The text of this book is set in 14.5-point Avenir Next LT Pro Regular.
The illustrations in this book were created digitally using Artstudio and Photoshop.

MANUFACTURED IN CHINA
10 9 8 7 6 5 4 3 2 1
First Edition

ONE TURTLE'S LAST STRAW

The Real-Life Rescue That Sparked a Sea Change

Written by **Elisa Boxer**   Illustrated by **Marta Álvarez Miguéns**

Crown Books for Young Readers
New York

The boy sucks up the last drops of drink through his straw.
After one more satisfied slurp, he tosses the cup in the trash.

Heavy winds come whipping by . . .
lifting the cup out of the trash can . . .
swirling it in the air . . .
smashing it to the ground . . .
sending it spinning down the street . . .
until it stops
in a storm drain.

The straw slips into the sewer.

Underground,
it meanders for miles
through a maze of steel pipes,
then spits out into a stream,
winding its way to the ocean.

In that same ocean, a sea turtle soars.

His front flippers fly him through the water with long,
sweeping strokes.

Until . . . a trawler net!
TRAPPED!

Dragged along the ocean floor, he starts to run out of air.
He needs to get back to the surface to breathe, or he will drown.
TANGLED!

Each furious flap of his flippers only wraps more rope around his shell.

He twists.

He turns.

One flipper comes free!

But the other is still stuck.

Gasping now.

Not much air left.

Struggling. Spinning.

Spinning. Unwinding!

He wriggles free just in time!
Right before running out of oxygen, he
speeds up to the surface to fill his lungs
with a full breath.

Freedom.
Fresh air.
Finally.

Hungry after his harrowing escape, the turtle dives down
to the ocean floor to find food.
   Crunch!

His sharp beak snags a crab scuttling across the seabed.

Satisfied, he swallows his catch.
Along with it, he slurps up a mouthful of seawater, which,
as usual, flows up and out his nose.

But something gets stuck.

Cough!

Something hard.

Cough! Cough!

Something he accidentally gobbled up along with the crab.

Cough! Cough! Cough!

He tries to throw it up, but he gags and chokes.
Part of the object is wedged up his nose.
The other part is stuck down his throat.
He can barely breathe!

He begins to lose his sense of smell, which he needs
to find food.
For weeks, he struggles to eat,
struggles to breathe,
struggles to survive.

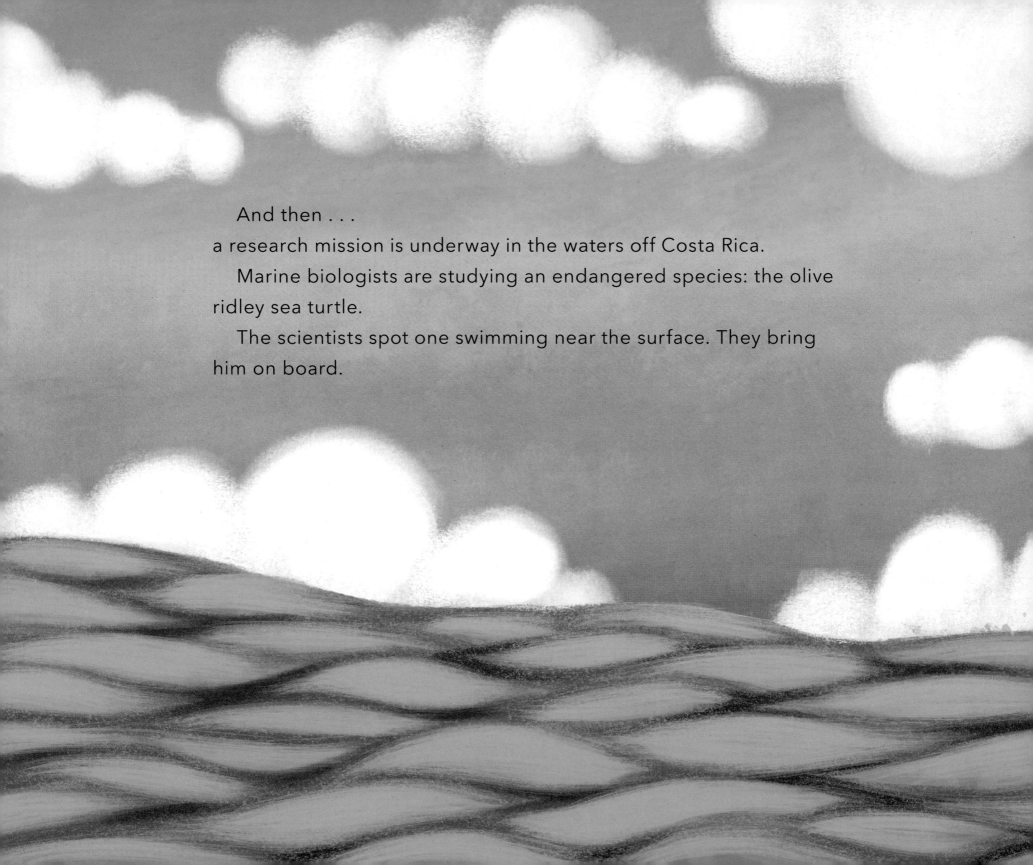

And then . . .

a research mission is underway in the waters off Costa Rica.

Marine biologists are studying an endangered species: the olive ridley sea turtle.

The scientists spot one swimming near the surface. They bring him on board.

He has something sticking out of his nostril. A barnacle, maybe?

Dr. Nathan Robinson, one of the researchers, takes out a pair of pliers.
He twists the object, trying to pry it loose.

But it's not a barnacle.

He pulls.

"I don't want to pull too hard," says Nathan. "I don't know what it's attached to!"

It's in deeper than they thought.

Had it hooked into the turtle's brain?

"A worm?" one of them wonders.

The turtle starts squirming and sneezing.

Out comes a small section of what looks like a stick, and the turtle squeezes his eyes shut in pain.

The researchers snip off a sample of the stick and examine it.

They see faded stripes.

"Don't tell me it's a straw!" says Dr. Christine Figgener, a marine biologist who's spent her career studying sea turtles.

She's also been trying to warn the world about plastic products and how they can hurt marine life.

It can't be a straw, she thinks as she films the scene with her phone.

They keep pulling.

The turtle hisses and winces, and a trickle of blood spills out of his nose and falls on the floor of the boat.

"I'm so sorry, baby," Christine says.

They pull out another inch.

They see the turtle struggling, but they know they're saving his life.

They pull some more.

At last, all four inches of the object come out.

The turtle opens his eyes.

He stops squirming,

stops sneezing,

stops hissing.

He starts breathing freely.

It's a plastic straw.

No one on the boat has ever seen anything like this.
They stop the bleeding, make sure the sea turtle is safe,
and set him free.
His front flippers fly him through the water with long, sweeping,
satisfied strokes.

In silence,
they watch him swim away.

Many months later, at a restaurant halfway around the world, a girl and her mother place an order.
The server starts toward the kitchen.
But then, the girl remembers something. A video.
She stops the server.
"I'll skip the straw," she says.

AFTERWORD

As a marine biologist who studies and protects sea turtles, I have seen the pain and suffering that plastic pollution has inflicted on marine wildlife. A few years ago our research team documented our removal of a plastic straw stuck in a sea turtle's nose in a video that has now been viewed more than 150 million times. We were able to save this one particular turtle, but how many more animals are suffering because of plastic?

My turtles don't have a voice, but I do, and I will continue to speak on their behalf and fight so they have a chance to live in a plastic-free ocean.

I truly hope that the turtle in the video didn't suffer in vain but that it motivates us all to think about our options and to choose to be inconvenienced rather than use a plastic straw, single-use plastic cutlery, or a styrofoam container.

You can be a part of the solution and help protect our friends in the ocean. The next time you think about using a single-use plastic product, ask yourself, "Is this really necessary?"

Thanks for being an Ocean Hero!

—Christine Figgener, PhD
Marine Conservation Biologist
(seaturtlebiologist.com)

Andrey MacCarthy

AUTHOR'S NOTE

There have been more than 150 million views of the video showing the turtle rescue that inspired this book. You can search for "the sea turtle with the straw in its nostril (short version)" or go to: youtube.com/watch?v=4MPHbpmP6_I.

When I interviewed Dr. Christine Figgener about the sea turtle's struggle, she told me she'd seen plastic bags inside turtles' stomachs and even a baby turtle stuck inside a plastic bottle. But never a sea turtle with a straw lodged inside its nasal cavity. She believes the turtle swallowed the straw thinking it was food, and it got stuck when he tried to regurgitate it. Based on the condition of the straw, she said it was likely lodged there for several weeks.

Dr. Figgener emphasized how, even in landlocked communities, straws can blow into storm drains and streams, then find their way into oceans. Studies estimate as many as 8.3 billion straws litter the earth's shorelines.

Dr. Nathan Robinson, the scientist who pulled the straw from the turtle's nose, told me his first feeling was guilt. "I had used plastic straws before, so I felt the responsibility for this turtle's plight partly sat on my shoulders," he said. But after the video went viral, his guilt turned to hope.

"I soon realized that people did not want to live in a world of single-use plastics," Dr. Robinson said. "We started to build the anti-pollution movement because we knew that by protecting our oceans, we were protecting our future."

While it's upsetting to think that one casual act of using a plastic bag, spoon, or straw can have such a devastating impact on marine life, the good news is that each of us has the power to change the world through our choices.

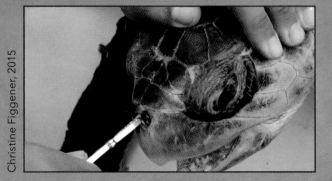

Pulling the straw from the sea turtle's nostril

Christine Figgener, 2015

The straw after removal

Nathan J. Robinson, 2015

KIDS TAKING ACTION TO TACKLE OCEAN POLLUTION

In 2010, in order to reduce waste, nine-year-old Milo Cress from Vermont asked the owner of a local restaurant to stop automatically putting straws in drinks and instead offer them as an option. Leunig's Bistro took him up on it and became the first restaurant in the country to use this "offer first" straw policy. Milo's action ultimately led to Vermont adopting this same policy statewide.

In 2018, twelve-year-old Chloe Mei Espinosa of Southern California was moved to action after watching the video of the sea turtle and the straw. She created her own website, skiptheplasticstraw.com, and convinced her Newport-Mesa Unified School District to get rid of plastic straws at each of its thirty-two campuses.

Also in 2018, twelve-year-old Anna Du of Massachusetts became so concerned with ocean pollution, she invented a Remote-Operated Vehicle (ROV) with an infrared camera, to detect microplastics on the ocean floor. The sixth grader also wrote a children's book, *Microplastics and Me,* to increase awareness about the plastics pollution problem. She has raised thousands of dollars to give free copies of her book to children and libraries in low-income communities.

"When I first started doing science fairs, I had no idea that a young girl without lots of money and just a little advanced engineering knowledge could make a difference in the world," Anna said. "I truly love working on a problem that's so much larger than me."

Pei Zhang

Anna Du with her microplastics-detecting ROV

BIBLIOGRAPHY

INTERVIEW

Figgener, Christine, PhD, marine biologist, in discussion with the author via telephone and email, August 2019.

Robinson, Nathan J., PhD, marine biologist, in discussion with the author via email, July 2021.

VIDEO

Sea Turtle Biologist. "The Sea Turtle with a Straw in Its Nostril—No to Single Use Plastics." (Shortened version) YouTube, August 10, 2015. Video, 3:47. youtube.com/watch?v=4MPHbpmP6_I.

ARTICLES

Cuda, Heidi Siegmund, and Elizabeth Glazner. "The Turtle That Became the Anti-Plastic Straw Poster Child." Plastic Pollution Coalition, November 11, 2015. plasticpollutioncoalition.org/blog/2015/10/27/the-turtle-that-became-the-anti-plastic-straw-poster-child.

Lee, Jane J. "How Did Sea Turtle Get a Straw Up Its Nose?" *National Geographic,* August 17, 2015. nationalgeographic.com/news/2015/08/150817-sea-turtles-olive-ridley-marine-debris-ocean-animals-science/.

Robinson, Nathan J., and Christine Figgener. "Plastic Straw Found Inside the Nostril of an Olive Ridley Sea Turtle." *Marine Turtle Newsletter* 147, 2015. seaturtle.org/mtn/archives/mtn147/mtn147-3.shtml?Nocount.

Rosenbaum, Sophia. "She Recorded That Heartbreaking Turtle Video. Here's What She Wants Companies Like Starbucks to Know About Plastic Straws." *TIME,* July 17, 2018. time.com/5339037/turtle-video-plastic-straw-ban/.

Sea Turtle Conservancy. "Information About Sea Turtles, Their Habitats, and Threats to Their Survival." conserveturtles.org/information-about-sea-turtles-their-habitats-and-threats-to-their-survival/.

U.S. Fish & Wildlife Service. North Florida Ecological Services Office. "Olive Ridley Sea Turtle." February 7, 2018. fws.gov/northflorida/SeaTurtles/Turtle%20Factsheets/olive-ridley-sea-turtle.htm.

EXPLORE FURTHER

BOOKS

Du, Anna. *Microplastics and Me.* Boston: Tumblehome, Inc., 2019.

French, Jess. *What a Waste: Trash, Recycling, and Protecting Our Planet.* New York: DK Children, 2019.

Layton, Neal. *A Planet Full of Plastic.* London: Wren & Rook, 2019.

Newman, Patricia. *Plastic, Ahoy! Investigating the Great Pacific Garbage Patch.* Minneapolis: Millbrook Press, 2014.

ONLINE RESOURCES

National Geographic. "Kids Take Action Against Ocean Plastic." Short Film Showcase. YouTube, February 21, 2017. Video, 4:26. youtube.com/watch?v=hKFV9IquMXA.

Plastic Pollution Coalition. "How to Talk to Your Kids About Plastic Pollution: Cartoons, Books, and Activities to Involve the Whole Family." plasticpollutioncoalition.org/blog/2018/5/3/how-to-talk -to-your-kids-about-plastic-pollution-cartoons-books-and-activities-to-involve-the-whole-family.

SEE Turtles. "Ocean Plastic & Sea Turtles." seeturtles.org/ocean-plastic.

Shaw, Allyson. "Kids vs. Plastic: Plastic Pollution: What's the Problem?" *National Geographic Kids.* kids.nationalgeographic.com/explore/nature/kids-vs-plastic/pollution/.

World Wildlife Fund. "What Do Sea Turtles Eat? Unfortunately, Plastic Bags." worldwildlife.org/stories/what-do-sea-turtles-eat-unfortunately-plastic-bags.